Anarcha Speaks

THE NATIONAL POETRY SERIES

The National Poetry Series was founded in 1978 to ensure the publication of five poetry books annually through five participating publishers. Publication is funded annually by the Lannan Foundation, Amazon Literary Partnership, Barnes & Noble, the Poetry Foundation, the PG Family Foundation and the Betsy Community Fund, Joan Bingham, Mariana Cook, Stephen Graham, Juliet Lea Hillman Simonds, William Kistler, Jeffrey Ravetch, Laura Baudo Sillerman, and Margaret Thornton. For a complete listing of generous contributors to the National Poetry Series, please visit www.nationalpoetryseries.org.

2017 COMPETITION WINNERS

The Lumberjack's Dove
GennaRose Nethercott
Chose by Louise Gluck for Ecco

Anarcha Speaks
Dominique Christina
Chosen by Tyehimba Jess for Beacon Press

feeld
Jos Charles
Chosen by Fady Joudah for Milkweed Editions

What It Doesn't Have to Do With
Lindsay Bernal
Chosen by Paul Guest for University of Georgia Press

Museum of the Americas
J. Michael Martinez
Chosen by Cornelius Eady for Penguin Books

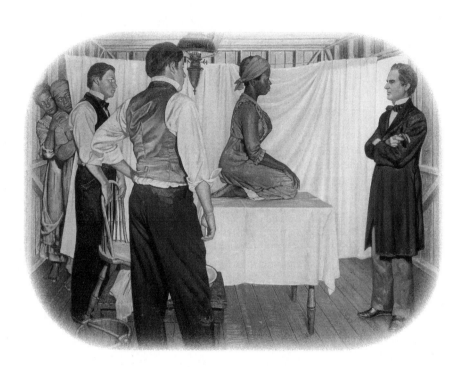

Anarcha
Speaks

· · · · · · · · · · · · ·

DOMINIQUE CHRISTINA

Beacon Press
Boston

BEACON PRESS
Boston, Massachusetts
www.beacon.org

Beacon Press books
are published under the auspices of
the Unitarian Universalist Association of Congregations.

21 20 19 18   8 7 6 5 4 3 2 1

This book is printed on acid-free paper that meets the uncoated paper
ANSI/NISO specifications for permanence as revised in 1992.

Text design and composition by Kim Arney

Frontispiece: Illustration of Dr. J. Marion Sims with "Anarcha,"
from the series "A History of Medicine in Pictures," by Robert
Thom, 1961. Courtesy of the Pearson Museum, with permission
from the Southern Illinois University School of Medicine.

Library of Congress Cataloging-in-Publication Data

Names: Dominique Christina, author. | Jess, Tyehimba, editor, writer of foreword.
Title: Anarcha speaks : a history in poems / Dominique Christina ;
selected by Tyehimba Jess ; introduction by Tyehimba Jess.
Description: Boston : Beacon Press, 2018. | Series: The National poetry series
Identifiers: LCCN 2017058986 (print) | LCCN 2018006046 (ebook) |
ISBN 9780807009314 (ebook) | ISBN 9780807009215 (paperback)
Subjects: LCSH: African American women—Poetry. | Women slaves—Poetry. |
Sims, J. Marion (James Marion), 1813-1883—Poetry. | Gynecologists—United
States—Poetry. | Human experimentation in medicine—Poetry. | Gynecology—
History—Poetry. | American poetry—African American authors. | BISAC:
POETRY / American / African American. | HISTORY /
United States / 19th Century.
Classification: LCC PS3604.O4655 (ebook) |
LCC PS3604.O4655 A83 2018 (print) |
DDC 811/.6—dc23
LC record available at https://lccn.loc.gov/2017058986

CONTENTS

Foreword by Tyehimba Jess · xi

Section I: She Is a Woman Therefore She Remembers
Anarcha Will Speak and It Will Be So · 3
Ghosts I Got · 4
The Preacher Give Us the Story of Job · 6
Benediction · 7
Massa's House · 8
Don't Wanna Hear It But · 9
From a Star I See Everything · 12
Black Gold · 13
The Chil'ren Might Know · 15
They Bringin in More · 17
Anarcha Feels Movement · 18
One Boy Named Montgomery · 19
Lucy Made a Girl · 20
She Need Help I Caint Manage It · 21
The Unquenchable Season · 22
Pronounce Me Lord · 23
I Shoulda Known Heaven First · 25
When I Get There · 26
She Got Further Than Anybody · 28
Conjure · 30
I Prove · 32

Massa Wants to Know · 34

A Powerful Spell · 35

Alabama but I Don't Know It · 36

The Missus, Big with Somebody Too · 37

What Do It Take · 38

Danger on the Other Side · 40

Little Bird Don't Know Nuthin · 42

This Time It Hurts · 43

Anarcha Dreams, OR How You Know You Ain't Gone · 45

the midwife is no midwife · 46

The Drowned Boy, Call Him John · 47

The Doctor by Now · 48

Marion Sims, the Doctor · 49

Anarcha Makes Milk Anyway · 52

Dr. Sims Comes Back, Makes an Offer · 53

Anarcha Will Leave in the Morning · 54

The Etymology of Anarchy · 56

Doctor/Massa Wants More · 57

Section II: The Juxtaposition of Experience

Blood Misbehaves: One Surgery as Anarcha Sees It · 61

Blood Misbehaves: The Surgery as Dr. Sims Sees It · 63

Not Dead but . . . · 64

How Doctor Sims Sees His Work · 65

How Anarcha Sees His Work · 66

Dr. Sims Makes Something New · 67

When the Quiver Stops, Ain't No Jesus · 68

Dr. Sims Will Buy 9 More   ·   69

Anarcha, in Position   ·   70

Dr. Sims Explains   ·   71

Flicker   ·   72

Dr. Sims Comes Clean   ·   73

Anarcha, Anarcha Come On Out . . .   ·   75

New Gals, No Good   ·   78

Things Past Tellin . . .   ·   80

A Wizard and His Magic, Nothing More   ·   82

No Magic, No How   ·   83

The Doctor Figures It Out   ·   85

The Doctor Gives Her Opium After   ·   86

Conniption   ·   87

First Is Last: How the Doctor Sees It   ·   89

First Is Last: How Anarcha Sees It   ·   91

A Dedication   ·   93

FOREWORD

A few weeks before sitting down to write this foreword, a cadre of Black women activists were successful in leading a long campaign to remove a statue of J. Marion Sims from the Manhattan streets by Central Park, where for decades he was honored as the "Father of Gynecology." Sims wrote his legacy of healing in the blood of enslaved Black women who had no choice but to surrender to his scalpel and thread, who endured his harrowing research only to be relegated to the footnotes of history.

> *"800 dollar mule 800 dollar mule"*
> that what massa say
> over the loud i make wit blood.

Dominique Christina plunges deep into a cauldron of searing ancestral voices to give us this arsenal of poems, voices, testimonies, and dreams that have been waiting to stretch and wail to us in this twenty-first century. She brings us the story of Anarcha, thought to be one of the main subjects of Marion Sims's bloody, painful experiments that cemented his reputation in the field of gynecology. Anarcha and eleven other slave women were Sims's subjects—their bodies volunteered by their masters.

> massa yellin 'bout:
> *what us gon do wit a nigga gal caint keep her own water* and
> *800 dollar mule! i paid 800 dollars for this mule for what?*

Branded expendable by virtue of their gender and race, Sims also believed these qualities rendered Black women impervious to pain. Anarcha and her fellow subjects bore the price of scientific progress with stitch after painful stitch at the core of their beings. Sims subjected Anarcha to thirteen experimental surgeries—all without anesthetic—to perfect his treatment of vesicovaginal and rectovaginal fistulas.

> *doctor don't do slaving like regular folk*
> *he built soft, like somethin young*
> *he don't yell much/ always readin*
> *put his fingers in you like nothin*
> *push on yo stomach/ make you squat*
> *then write it down.*

In these poems, we witness the poet weaving in and out of the most intimate injuries with inquiries in search of answers only the body can provide. From fertility to pregnancy, from delivery to debridement, Dominique Christina takes us beyond the mere medical witness of these women's bodies and into their tapestry of dream and desire. With masterful use of image and an ear for language that haunts and glows in poem after poem, the poet has delivered us from one century to another in conversation with the spirit of Anarcha.

And when we read her story, of forced labor and torturous experiments that resulted in gynecological treatments still in practice, we are elegantly and ruthlessly reminded of gender and racial inequities that dog our nation to this day. According to the Centers for Disease Control and Prevention, Black women are three to four times more likely to die of pregnancy or delivery complications than white women.

This poet's ability to capture voices from the past that ring true to the present is a gift that we need to listen to carefully today. Not only because the voices bring urgent parable and insight from the frontline between degradation and spirit in the nineteenth century but also because of the richness, depth, and uncompromising humanity with which these poems are written and this singular story is told. A story that, in its telling, lets us know in no uncertain terms:

heaven must be insurrection.

—TYEHIMBA JESS

Anarcha Speaks

She Is a Woman
Therefore She Remembers

Anarcha Will Speak and It Will Be So

massa come in like he know i caint cry
new tears

he take what he want
he keep a hot hand

every new hatred
cinch my throat closed.

he *take* me

give me a name made outta iron
he say it til i ain't myself

i, sheet rock.
i, a salted wound.

i the upset of everything,
unholy,
　　　　this.

Ghosts I Got

ain't got god enough
to leave me even a minute
for myself

all the folk in
front of me and behind me
the ones kneelin next to me
sufferin the same sun
i see em all and my own self too

we bottom of the boat heavy heavy
we swayin in our own shit and vomit
caint stop it
we rollin over each other
we cry out
we bribe god or whatever listenin
we shackled in the deep
we losin everything

these ghosts i got
like to remember
like to wallop me
won't let none of it leave

i turn against myself
caint find my own feet
under all this mud
all these graves
all that ocean
tryin to know me

i say *get off me*
but nothin gets lighter
i bottom of the boat heavy heavy
i drownin always
i floatin and flailin and
losin my prayers

these ghosts i got
got too many names
too many tongues

I dizzy from listenin to em   all.

THE PREACHER GIVE US THE STORY OF JOB

i wanna hear it right but
seem like god always
takin somethin
and wantin somethin
all at once and all you
can do is call it his will

like this one time
massa grab a boy named Clink
tie him to the sycamore
     the one hang heavy
        in june and
flay him for no reason
'cept to show us we could
give our blood to
them branches too

he do it easy cuz he can
just like god and we
gotta stand there and
watch the leaves
shiver from the spill
of this boy and be
thankful it ain't us.

far as I can feel it
Job ain't nothin but
a workday wit massa.

the only thing promised
is the bleedin.

BENEDICTION

got a rhythmic dread now
cuz in spite of myself
i been prayin and tryna
see will god show up
but you pay for that
kinda faithfulness
wit sorrow when
don't nothin move
and massa still massa
and all you got
is the ugly of the world
and your own dumb wish
that light could get in
and you get where you
could punch a hole in
the sky and
wear your enemy's teeth
around your neck and
never believe in nothin
again not god not
prayer not tomorrow
but then what i got
what chance i got to
slip outta this dream
long enough to
try a savior and see
do he believe in me
enough to come by here?

MASSA'S HOUSE

noiseless as a grave

the missus caint get an egg to

fry right she need

lemons in the water

lace on the table

fruits sittin heavy in big ole

glass bowls

i takes the brown ones

stick em in my apron

juice run down like church

pulp-sweet and hidden

the missus don't know

how to keep the soup pots full.

she sick wit lovelessness

she preach. she beat

til she think she got somethin

she can use.

but me?

i thick. i thick wit secrets . . .

only thing i got that's mine.

Don't Wanna Hear It But

betsey say when you don't
find no blood 'tween
yo legs you   *expecting*
and I'm askin what i'm
sposed to be waitin on and
she say a baby and my heart
give out cuz i don't mean
to be nobody's mammy
on account of bein cursed and
unspecial who want a mama
wit all them demons
'round her neck but betsey say
get ready girl get ready
and i share myself wit
the kinda sadness
that don't belong to nothin
on this earth

what massa did to me
i do not say
i disremember the
hooch on his
breath on my face
them hands
'round my throat
up my skirt
the stink of him
on everythin
pinned down and

moanin into myself
couldn't even unhitch
a scream cuz
his face too close
to my face
his whiskers
chafe my cheek
splinter my back
the wood shed
was sposed to keep
all this to itself so
no i don't recall
what massa did

but

when he left
seem like he stayed
like i kept
some of it
like i ain't
have no other way

and now Betsey say
i *expecting* . . .

how you translate
a bludgeonin to
a birth?

you tell me how
i'm sposed to
do that—

a baby.
from the mud pile . . .
a baby . . .

one more
thing i don't
know how to carry.

FROM A STAR I SEE EVERYTHING

one night we slip out
slick as paste and quiet
nighttime stubborn
keep a heat anyhow
sky blurred wit fever
i sweat my kerchief loose

we layin out
we lookin up

we shook wit night wind
we knees up, drift wood.

i say:
what you make a dem stars?
he say:

they just like us.   sizzlin   dead.

Black Gold

"To be sold: a choice cargo of 250 fine healthy NEGROES, just arrived from the Windward & Rice Coast. The utmost care has already been taken, and shall be continued, to keep them free from the least danger of being infected with the SMALL-POX . . ."

slavers say we black gold

highest price for the ones

who make it well enough

to suicide they own longing

to lift and tote

we keeps the rice and sugar

comin up *up*

sets by the fire

seed out the cotton

gin it bale it do it over

raffle us off

sarah, mulatto, good cook

make the bread like they like it.

dennis her son. he fix a horse

to ride, ride.

fanny good with french words

do hair, seamstress too.

dandridge, mulatto, he a carpenter

like jesus, paint too.

nancy his wife (they say)

black as coal.

she wash, she iron, she talk

it sound like birds.

mary ann, creole

no spine yet.

they beat her she go soft

as butter.

and fanny and emma and betsey, lucy and me.

a hungry territory

of ocean, snatched.

THE CHIL'REN MIGHT KNOW

we once was warriors
bone sharp and tangling up
wit whatever wild was in the world
before some ships rolled in
wit folk we ain't never seen
brandin iron and bullet men
claimin everythin
leavin misery

maybe
they know we ain't always
been so lowly
so feverish wit brokenness
so in fil   trated
maybe they can look past

the bruises
to see when we
were bigger underneath
and forgive us our frailty
we was overcome
wit the kind of
meanness that don't care
about nothin but
feedin itself

we had hands once
and a river to bathe in

and names
full names
that called us home.

the chil'ren might know that
if they lookin at us right

we lost our mouths
'cross a mighty mighty ocean.
coulda died but we don't know how . . .

They Bringin in More

one boy busted so bad
his lip, a wind chime
at his chin

        i think lawd what now
        the girl so young no hair
        'tween her legs
        she remind me of the plums
        we pulped for bread.

massa go in a wagon

        come back wit more
        whip em straight out
        so they know him

the missus eat sugar cubes
at the gate.
we the bleedin yolk.
a congregation of ruin(ed).

        we watch.

ANARCHA FEELS MOVEMENT

midwife say my belly droopin
wit a boy

she say she see it
by how i carry low,
like apologizin for
somethin i ain't did yet.

massa tell the missus i need
extra meat

the missus suck her teeth
bloody my mouth

she know i got somethin
unblessed wit me

one day i feels him
kick and think:

you hangin on huh?

One Boy Named Montgomery

come from 'cross the river
lookin fo a girl he call hisself
marryin get caught and massa keep him
he brown as mud
one arm don't work
from the dogs

pulled him out the tree
by his elbow they tell me
he moanin they chewin
til massa satisfied
he go by Montgomery
he say
his name mean he come
from some place.

what my name say 'bout *me*?

Lucy Made a Girl

she lookin like massa
too much for the missus
and we know it
great god we know it

so when massa come in
creepin midnight low to
snatch that baby right
off lucy teet
and she hollerin and pleadin
sayin no massa no not my baby
and massa swat her mouth shut
and say it ain't yo baby
i roll over and close my eyes

slip into numbness
cuz ain't no stayin
not here
and ain't no keepin nothin
but lucy forgot all that

and what she get for the sin of
tryin to love somethin?
a baby she made but don't own
a mouth full of blood
and massa cussin her
for how she grieve.

She Need Help I Caint Manage It

it ain't like we knew it before we saw it.
she young, her mouth don't
keep to itself.
she burn the bread,
talk when the missus come in,
we ain't used to this kinda foolishness
from no young gal
so we shadows
we moonless, waitin til massa
show her who he is.

when the lash open her back up
the day goes back to what it's been
all this time 'fore she come here
swingin words 'round
til we dizzy.
she say *try* and *tomorrow*
like them words belong to her,
she say *try* and *tomorrow*
and we forget the god they gave us.

THE UNQUENCHABLE SEASON

mornin not supple,

autumn got a handprint.

it rush out crisp, orange.

i don't wake up next to nobody.

lonely sometime til it wears me out

neck tight, unkissed.

i feed the chil'ren in the big house

and bite my own cheek

taste iron

a prank, you could call it,

the bleedin.

Pronounce Me Lord

or at least let me hear what
songs my own name got
when ain't no lash
swallowin and stealin
my mouth

closed shut melody
ruptured
no parables for
the dead or

the limbo of the livin

i want my name
wit lavender in it
a noonday dance
to call out the palm wine

the sugar
the hunger in my blood

i want my mama
to see me hurricane
these chains
these knotted joints

see me ripe
see me possible
see me pushin   up

from myself

i ain't never seen a sunrise without
a body in it

i want my name

my name lord,
one long dream
          of daylight.

I Shoulda Known Heaven First

not this house of stone and religion to die in every day the
midwife say my baby gon stay long enough in my belly
for the leaves to change wish he knew to stay put or get
gone wish he knew to not come wish he knew i caint be
his mammy and keep my hands. i shoulda got heaven first.
some far off not here pasture wit feathers and skyyyyy and
men wit smilin faces no powder burns no welted backs
churned yellow from sun, from heat i woulda liked to know
me as myself i'm big wit a son and bruised wit hell that don't
leave just cuz you call on jesus.

When I Get There

trouble gon be outta sight
i mean somethin magic

somethin smilin and
big wit the kinda sorcery

i glad to be undone by

o heaven you must be sweet
cuz massa caint find you

no sweet by and by
for the lash man and all the nastiness

he got

when i get there
i gon sit right down and

raise my knees
clap these hands

shout til the moon splits

o heaven you got space for me?
a spare room for a phantom?

i been hungry so long
famine my only song

i split by an ocean
i torn up by longing

when i get there to that great big house
i mean to look god dead in the face

show him my scars   my vacant heart   this blood corsage
and ask him   *why.*

SHE GOT FURTHER THAN ANYBODY

it don't matter what the preacher say
i got a heart, i can feel it.
it keeps a ache better than
anything else i got.
better than my back my hips
my arms two good legs
hands knuckles every godless bone.
i knowed she was runnin cuz i sent her
wit a yam pushed down in a croaker sack
leavin!
i seen it and said what prayers i could
she deserved a god from somewhere.
got as far as the river 'fore massa
found her and set them dogs out.
she give the babies her tit ev'ry evenin so
her milk runnin down like
rain water
them dogs bit her breasts
clean off

massa burn her right there at the bank
say she no mo good what wit no milk
and broken open.

she got further than anybody
i ain't never been far as the gate.
she took her own magic wit her they say.
she wasn't thinkin 'bout the big house or massa
jus' the river they say.
leavin!

i don't pray no mo
but i swear when it rain
it smell like sweet milk,
the blood   mixed in.

Conjure

sometimes
in the deep
of me
i writhe
i drill down into
my tears
strangle my
tongue
kill god
go huntin
deepening to
darkness
ash and ruin

i watch

from the pit
i sizzle
i   d
      r
        i
          f
            t
tattered
ready
moonsick
lettin evil
inhabit me

ride me
rush these bones
stun these eyes
i brave
i ready
i callin
on something
old
i conjure
i enter

steady
wantin everything
to bleed.

I Prove

i am five smooth stones
> my belly quake and hell

find me bleedin
> from 'tween my legs

i don't cry or
> say nothin

i am a creek bed
> the waves take me wit em

but i still me, more than i am it.
> i squallin invisible

til the midwife say:

somebody get me some water
this gal caint have the baby now

then the ice chips
> in my mouth on my forehead

mercy!
> feel so good i forget 'bout

the river i got

  midwife say: *pull him back up into you gal*

so i get like something hard.

  finally finally she say the trouble over it wasn't

nothin but the heat

  gives me more ice i

bite til my teeth a flight of stairs.

blood sometimes,

the river.

of me.

Massa Wants to Know

if what i did was plan it.
to pull at the salted edge
to get the boy out of me.
i say no massa i ain't did nothin but
my work when somethin got hot
in me we cooled it down massa
we cooled it right down
i ain't got no plans,
i say.
and jus' like dat i know
i could make some if i put my mind there.
what would it take to kill
somethin that ain't here yet?
got to be like murderin
a ghost or what the preacher
calls *the soul.*
ima go to church
listen on how.
jesus died,
do it like them Romans did,
easy.

A POWERFUL SPELL

this baby whatever it is
gon hafta be its own religion

       see that bird yonder imitatin spring?

winter gon find him all the same
plumed and shiverin.

       flirtin wit wind

here is what nobody knows

i ain't never loved nothin

not one thing
not the mornin cuz that's an axe blade
not the night cuz that's a murder
not the river cuz it ain't deep enough
not the folk i bleed wit
cuz they the same ruin
not tomorrow or today
or my own dumb will
cuz it's the noose 'round my neck
most days

       that bird is imitatin spring
       lookin for its own religion

this baby whatever it is
gon learn–

i wingless and loving, never.

ALABAMA BUT I DON'T KNOW IT

i was big wit a baby i couldn't name
when somebody tol' me
where we was at.
all i knew was the peach trees,
wet with sugar
mockingbird molten feathers
make a trail look like blood
i put a bucket over my head
to push out the heat
we sleep in til we ache for
rain that don't never come
no ways.
somebody say: *this here Alabama.*

don't mean nothin to me.
every name, somber
a hollowed out empty,

Alabama.

THE MISSUS, BIG WITH SOMEBODY TOO

Midwife say i ain't the only one

makin somethin

she say the missus been sick

and meanin it too . . .

doctor came

say she ain't bled in moons

got somethin comin

massa proud as Pilate

he done made himself

so many times he god or somebody

like it.

preacher say *vanity*

when you love

yoself more than you sposed to

massa got *vanity*

ev'ry time he see me

he think he here forever.

the missus a yellow shawl

her blood machinery

keep him feelin big.

i, the axe handle he swings

for spite.

What Do It Take

to climb out a body

i ask Montgomery

when he shuckin corn

and soft like he get sometimes

he say ain't much to death

he say folk go all the time

he say his own mammy

cut stripes in her arms

and found heaven in the time

it take to make cornbread

say she ain't cry or moan

just went right out like she planned—

see that bird yonder? (he say)

i see it (I say)

its own mammy left it

lookin for other sky

didn't care none about

the baby bird

chewin blind in its nest

when you love somethin

you can still leave it and go lookin

for other sky (he say)

death ain't much (he say)

he wanna know why i'm askin

i shrug, say

never mind it Montgomery

but now i know i got to

love me enough to leave

ain't that something?

i got to love *me* enough

to leave

that's the trouble . . .

DANGER ON THE OTHER SIDE

when folk run off from massa
ain't no god to keep em
from every havoc that ever was
that's the danger about hunger and
wantin somethin for yo'self
i know it all this time
i know it
one gal say hell is on the
other side of the gate
say she heard about wolves
keepin watch and a woman in the woods
wit a hex from not belongin to no place
say she live like animals do
cuz ain't no massa
so she liable for all her
own sorrow
another gal say massa keepin us
safe from junk men jus' waitin
to catch a woman on her own

to bleed her and make her to

do any awful thing they think up

she say we better off

wit massa cuz at least he

churched

she say the other side of

the gate is a hurt you don't wanna know

she say god want it like it is

she say ain't no winnin against

what god want

and i think:

god keep me embalmed, unmoving

god of the padlock god of the lash god of the bit and noose

who *he* answer to? who?

Little Bird Don't Know Nuthin

'bout this world he tryna enter

not one thing

about it

he fix hisself to my ribs

like a meal I ain't chew good

he kick he stretch

he dumb wit life and askin me

        me

to be more than these hands i got

little bird pick hisself a mama wit

no god left

and a pa wit hard hands, no heart

and all the time

i'm thinkin

why?

This Time It Hurts

the air crowdin in on me
too many hands and no
sky so i runnin.
little bird chew me *up*

i slip out from under *me*
go drownin.

this time it hurt *bad.*
i cracklin wit a ache that
snatch me, pull me under.
water over my head
my legs ain't mine
   what dis baby want wit me?
no room to die in
no heaven waitin
no flowers in my thighs.
   midwife here again.
she like the moon.
she come in wit the blood, yellin

push and no ice for my mouth.
i small and for all i know dyin
i breakin
water! empty handed
but killin everythin in the room
wit the flood i got

massa come in chewin brine
tell the midwife *get the boy out quick* and
stop all that goddamn blood ya hear me?

midwife tug from the inside
caint keep a hold a *me*
     steal away, steal away
     steal a way home.
     i ain't got long to stay here.
red.
red.
gone.

Anarcha Dreams, or How You Know You Ain't Gone

you ever see a boy get hisself trapped in a well?

(she ask me from inside my head)

        yes ma'am lil boy fell in last winter.

he get out on his own?

        no ma'am took a lotta pullin and rope.

uh huh. water wanna keep you.

        yes it do.

why you think you different?

        ma'am?

why you think you different?

        I ain't got that thought. i jus' sick is all.

you ain't sick. you a well. yo boy trapped inside. caint swim a lick.

        what i got to work wit?

not yo back or yo brains but yo heart will keep.

        am i dyin you reckon?

you *the well.* he *the drowned one.*

        i didn't mean to love him no how.

open your eyes.

open your eyes!

THE MIDWIFE IS NO MIDWIFE

she, the woman with curious blood.

deathbeds be acres wide

and absence can be renamed, always.

    she, the tourniquet.

    the one who bone and tendon, know.

    the one who delivered her own sold-off babies.

first a girl.

three boys after.

hoisted hips, the haystack hymnal.

pulling pulling

she named each one.

no more no more.

    everything trying to be born travels her hands.

    massa made it so.

    tickled from her ingenuity, the gristle.

every baby, bright as blood.

pulled from a dream.

you will be won,

(she thinks)

you will be won.

The Drowned Boy, Call Him John

remember to catch everything . . .
if he gone
don't leave me wit nothin
take it all from me
every part

i caint keep a drowned boy
in me i guess
so take it all from me
let the wind decide
what to do with his bones

i sigh wit two tongues.

ooze, gone-boy
yo mama is a well
to trap fish
to chew bone . . .

i mighta called you John (3:16)

THE DOCTOR BY NOW

it seem like i caint get over killin somethin

so i bleed, bleed.

sun crush everything underneath it

i caint keep cool

i shiver, *heat.*

i quake, *heat.*

midwife beat a paste

leg bone of a donkey

she use to beat and beat.

bay leaf

chamomile for rest

she ask the blood be still

but me?

a boat

no oar.

no captain

midwife tell massa i broke

where she caint fix it.

he say: *Git the doctor. Enough mess for that*

   . . . now.

Marion Sims, the Doctor

He, having matriculated from the Carolinas,
        brand new wife, two patients dead from
something wild he could not wrestle down.

Opens a hospital in Montgomery,
        the doors bore his name.
Amidst the sawmill sun-downs
the timber gang negroes, dust-bitten,
        hungry.

But he is a doctor.
A man who keeps with science.

He will go church-ward toward the plantation.
        He will see about the bleeding.
The slave girl who was torn up
        by her own son.

The stink of shit and sweat
The county was famous for,
        The hoof and wheel tracks marrying
Under his unhurried shoes.

A thick gall when he sees her.

       (He swallows it down.)

This gal is a cave of sudden ruin.

          Labia stretched like a howling mouth.

Only thing to do is close the wound,

       (he wagers)

All doctors know *that* much.

She is open all over.

Her upflung hips, everything unhinged

        Silent, silent like she is trying

to invent reasons for breathing.

The primal *inertia!*

        Save for some mewling gal in the corner

Swaddling the baby he drags out, already swollen, going blue.

He shuts what doors he can.

        Takes the thread. Needles the pink.

Her eyes roll around her head like marbles.

Back in the morning, he tells the

Bleeding negro woman.

I'll getcha fixed up good, you watch.

He says it like ambition.

Anarcha Makes Milk Anyway

"800 dollar mule 800 dollar mule"
that what massa say
over the loud i make wit blood.
i caint keep it to myself
i worshippin somethin ugly
from the inside
it keep a watch over my legs
my back . . .
a well always gon be a well.
massa yellin 'bout:
what us gon do wit a nigga gal caint keep her own water   and
800 dollar mule! i paid 800 dollars for this mule for what?
i gets where i sittin straight up
make it look like keepin on.
just then, milk from these plain tits, milk!
lets down hot on my dress,
milk!
i makin nectar wit no baby

at *all*.

Dr. Sims Comes Back, Makes an Offer

by now, rain and winter.
i back in the kitchen on a busted stool
cannin tomatoes makin do
settin still on a pile a old rags
cuz i leaks now most all the time
terrible stink i keep, the missus see me, cuss me regular.

she made a baby, see?
wit no funk from dyin
i gives it my own milk sometimes when she say *get to it*
baby jus' nibble and keep confused.
don't never eat from his own mama.
she make a boy like i made jus' livin, see?

i pickling, i quiet
sun slippin in through the gray
catch my dress and hang on.

then here come massa say the doctor wanna take me off his
    hands
say he there to get me regular
fine. new hell, whatever.

Anarcha Will Leave in the Morning

seem like now i really *lookin*
at the big house, seein it like
i ain't been here the whole time.

like, what about them pecan trees
i pulled from since always?
what about the chamomile growin
wild as hoodoo under the porch
it come up,
we make a marmalade . . .
good too!

the pond out past the meat house
glow green after a good rain
mossy on the top
almost look like stuffing.
Montgomery get crawfish from
it sometime oohwee! we *eat*
and it feel like christmas.

you know, on christmas
the missus be in good spirits

she let us sing outright
she tellin us 'bout jesus birthday
and salvation and how gawd
might let a few of us in dem
pearly gates if we pray hard, ask for
him to look over our
hell-bitten flesh.

i leavin in the mornin
gon be wit the doctor.
i go out by the pond . . .
one las' look you know?
Montgomery there,
not smilin.
jus' point to a fat rock sittin
on some dirt, dark and wet as fudge.

there
(he say)
that there is where they buried yo baby.

THE ETYMOLOGY OF ANARCHY

1.
ruler-less.
without.
leader-less.
without.
chaos they say.
melted coin.
a shiny purse,
the seams pulled out.
at the end of all development,
death.
the individual, crushed
unless . . .

2.
Anarcha,
you are a house
of too many hands.
how else do
they build
but by blood?
by bone?

Doctor/Massa Wants More

seem like i grow a new mouth

when he come

wit them metal sticks

proddin me no better than

you do some tired mare

i *holler!* and it sound like smoke

he keep on, on

i give away my eyes.

this his work

(he say)

each word a land i

don't know about.

    fistula   hemorrhage   obstruction

i go away from my own self

pack up and leave

dis lunatic country of blood

i, a milked cow

the salted meat

doctor/massa don't never get full.

The Juxtaposition of Experience

Blood Misbehaves: One Surgery as Anarcha Sees It

new big house new missus
lucy and betsey in the wagon wit me.
the doctor want us to hisself.
he vex we caint shut up the piss, the blood.

    and me like a dog

    panting ugly, make me 'shamed.

    steam comin thick from under my dress.

    we get there.

sycamore trees leanin
from rot, a few sad cows
back legs pink and hairless
mules, chickens, pigs,
barn need paint, but big.

    doctor don't do slaving like regular folk

    he built soft, like somethin young

    he don't yell much/ always readin

put his fingers in you like nothin
push on yo stomach/ make you squat
then write it down.

    we in the barn learnin how morning

    happens wit this new doctor/massa . . .

then he say: *Anarcha you go first*
and just like that
i comin out my dress like always.
figurin my knees out and
how to survive em when they used like feet.
betsey and lucy, next.
they know it so they forget their necks
sail their eyes away from me
comin apart comin apart . . .
it ain't funny but i see what i must look like from here.
black and swollen, horizontal to the world
like a line drawn in sand
you know hurt comin soon.
doctor/massa pokin me hard.
i hunched i heavin
i jus' a river for him to drown in.
he get mad i got *so much*
he see now.

blood, misbehaves.

Blood Misbehaves: The Surgery as Dr. Sims Sees It

The complication with the Negro
Is how robust they are.

They confuse you with their bleeding.

A trick of sorts.
A siren from the inside
But then you notice
They are holding on
Filled with a wild vigor
Something (perhaps) the jungle bequeathed.

I will teach them to quiet the blood.
The girl is too willful with it.

Robust though, this one.
She can take   *so*   *much*
More.

Not Dead but . . .

seem like it

this bruise ain't no girl
she gone
she never gon be again
she too much a ghost even
for burial

     ain't enough language

     for the hurt of me

     i mad at my own heartbeat

     shouldn't be no rhythm in my chest

     no steady tick and pulse

i caint quite figure leavin
but i ain't been here long

     you lookin at somethin

     god ain't got around to namin

     you lookin at flesh that is not flesh

     bones jinglin like wind chimes

in a house nobody stay in
how you kill a dead thing?
what kinda weapon work   on a ghost?

How Doctor Sims Sees His Work

These gals, with their ferocious insides,
Ooze and sweat and wake each morning
Trumpeting their blood
Blundered bodies strutting a losing argument

Betsey falls out the quickest
Lucy will whimper and move too much.
But Anarcha, the cougar-eyed gal
Split clean from end to end
Is where the work is.

I will learn the diabolical complexity
Of *woman*: a synonym for ruin.

How Anarcha Sees His Work

i seen a chicken get his head
cut off and bein a chicken
he dumb and don't know he
dead so he floppin and still runnin the yard
still! no head at all blood like bread crumbs
runnin runnin and folk laugh and
wait on the chicken to know he gone and it
take a while

i mean it ain't always quick or easy
for a dead thing to know it's a dead thing
so it's squawkin and flappin
like it still got life and ain't no life there
at all and *that* is what it's like.

doctor/massa tickled
at the blood and the squawkin
waitin on me to know i'm a dead thing
and me, dumb wit stayin.

Dr. Sims Makes Something New[*]

What should happen, most always, is invention.

There is no wider mystery in the universe than that of woman,

What salt and bone she's got.

She is a composition of afterthought.

A borrowed rib, if you know your Bible.

She is so easily *disassembled*.

I take the ruined stock of Eve,

The wilted petals, the spent flesh,

And bring it wire, steel.

Restoration.

Everything we delight in came

First by the blood of a woman

And then

And then

Iron and what men do

After.

---

[*] Using a pewter spoon and a complicated set of mirrors and lighting,
Marion Sims invents what will be the precursor to the modern-day
speculum, which is used in gynecological procedures to this day.

When the Quiver Stops, Ain't No Jesus

i know better but i'm thinkin:
kill me. kill me and be done wit it kill me killmekillmekillme
doctor/massa makin science 'tween my legs
i, wordless and wantin heaven . . .
even hell
least i be gone from snatchin hands
i shiver like winter
betsey and lucy there too
we each, crouchin in a corner
ignorin the other one's burnin

this about bein black and woman too.
i think of the preacher
who say Jesus wept forty days and nights
by hisself
i pray what i know
i ask the quiver to stop
when it do,
still

ain't no Jesus.

Dr. Sims Will Buy 9 More

That morning he woke up and coupled
With his wife unceremoniously threw a leg
Over the bed after, sat up and told her
What they needed was more negroes
Like sayin you need to pick up milk from the store
Like sayin you outta eggs and corn meal
It was a simple thing you know . . .

The statement and the weightlessness
Of it like a shrug or a wink

More women like the other three
Ruined somehow from the inside

His house would be a city of resurrection maybe
Or medical marvel . . .

Every time you see a black girl bleeding
Think: *Progress.*

ANARCHA, IN POSITION

alright gal get the water from your eyes pull your knees up
keep your feet flat be still.

me? a bruised ghost
i concentrate on
my teeth/ the roof of my mouth/
i'm tryna rub it smooth/ concentrate on not blinkin

see how long I can go til my eyes need to shut.

doctor/massa again. he fancy wit his mind
always tryin a new thing
so i give away all my pink, scuffed, wet

he say: *experiment.*

hurt the same.

Dr. Sims Explains

God is the scalpel

I wizard a suture

I sorcery a wound

Torn birds

Never meant to know sky,

I say *wings* and

Flight is the same as prayer.

Things die to make room

For miracle–

The ratio of Lazarus to grave.

Flicker

i came up outta sleep like a hen plucked and dressed for some
saturday night banquet to find doctor/massa pullin up my skirt
betsey and lucy pretend sleep like they don't
know nighttime ain't one revelation of evil after the next.

seem to me like doctor/massa take a church
and pull at it til ain't no heaven to look for at all/ just the blood
    beneath the stones
the busted knuckled blistered hands of some witless negro that
    put em up
the calluses and the want and the want and the *want*
you hear me lawd *the want* . . . that steams up from itself
a hiss that caint ever be a hymn

men don't care nuthin 'bout resurrection
not with womenfolk and the flesh we got for poundin . . .
a nail, a nail, for the sin of bein born.

Dr. Sims Comes Clean

When fierce with science and strategy

A man, a *doctor*,

Beset with a certain vigor and interest
In fleshly arithmetic
The insistent ritual of skin and bone,
An awful marriage indeed.
For what God would make so flimsy
A mask? Should there not be
Some sturdier place to encase
The *soul?* That elusive
Centerpiece of personhood?
That stone which mocks good reason . . .

I am not ordinary.
There is a great stir in me . . .
A heavy-handed ambition.
To feed it is all there is.
To be my own answered prayer.
To lift the accursed nature of woman . . .

To be a doctor, a good one,
Is to be Adam. The *first* to find his hands and call them hands.
To look for the geography of impossible
And travel there daily.
Despite the hearty arguments
Put upon us by doubt.

Ah, this. The Adam breed then.
The ones God neither loves nor envies.
We are the *same*, He and I.
Two engineers of flesh
Who will stare down the blood,
Dumb our eyes to piteous howl and pleas
In the advancement of our own autobiography . . .

What is a doctor but a God?
We both seek our names on everything.
You will know, by who has lived,

And you will know by **who has died**, that we were   here.

Anarcha, Anarcha Come On Out . . .

sun tryna scald everything so we
don't hardly move
just sets under the sycamore
waitin on an ending of any kind.

lucy been silly wit herself all day
cuz a boy Massa-Doctor call Hitch
(on account of he take care of the horses and wagon)
done messed around and made her feel somethin real
so she actin like Massa-Doctor ain't
killin us every day.

i tell you he open that black bag and i
give God my right eye.
i mean, i *leave* . . . out my own self,
my own body i just leave til he done
cuz pain is a house you caint never get the
door closed on when he start up wit doctorin
i be tryin to remember Jesus but
somebody gotta tell me why
all I get for prayers is a river 'tween
my legs and nobody to hold me, ever

i hear lucy say she love Hitch and
somethin in me catch on a hook and
go down.

what you mean 'love'?
don't see how.
ain't you gotta know something 'bout yo own unbroken heart to feel it?

i caint even tell you 'bout my own mama.
she got sold off soon's she had me.
pulled me right off her tit so who can say
bout love?! what nigga you know
can tell you the shape of it?
huh? love a land we hear about
but don't never get to visit

i caint say what bein held is like . . .
i loveless and starved
two unsung breasts

but the subject is lucy
and how she think she *love* Hitch
and i'm sayin no way
preacher say God so L O V E D the world he gave his son
and that sound like something you gotta
be free to feel . . .
but when she go glitterin off behind him

i think of Ole Biddy
then my own dead baby
out back of the meat house

by the pond wit the green moss on top
and Montgomery catchin crawdads
and how it woulda been nice maybe
to love somebody
to feel it come back
not mockin
not wit its head down
but to *feel* it
and go glitterin off after somebody
who wouldn't never raise my skirt
without askin first.

NEW GALS, NO GOOD

You cannot get ready for the heat
Of Alabama and the hummingbirds
The whoosh of occasional wind
And mumbling negroes picking and
Pulling and crumbling in front of a trough
Each night to slurp cornbread and buttermilk
Without washing the red dirt from
Their hands . . . savage and
Comforting in its simplicity.

I caught two little ones
Robbing a bird's nest in the orchard
Their love-starved eyes
Matched only, in want, by their sunken bellies.
I knew they needed the rod,
Being children and negro
Discipline is a necessary hot hand.
It should come with no hesitation, the lash.
But here now, I am tuckered out from
Gals whose silly wombs ooze and bleed willfully,
The stink of stillborn babies
Spilling out of them,
Each day a new steam from
Beneath their skirts.

I have purchased three new ones.
Not so worn out as the others.
They will need to be broken open
Before my hands can know them properly.

There is no science to discover
In flesh that has not been torn,
And torn . . . asunder.

THINGS PAST TELLIN . . .

somethin no bigger than a whimper
got in me where i couldn't reach it
or lay it flat.
somethin like a curse God give me
when i ain't lookin til it catch a hold a me
and make me disturb my own stayin.

way I figure, i been prayin and prayin
for a *way*.
some kinda redemption carved out
for a nigga woman wit a busted up womb
a gone-baby and the spill of him
still clutterin up my insides.
prayin prayin for God for *anybody* to
snatch me out this hot
and put some light on me for always.

but ain't nobody showed up and now i think about
that time it got so dry the crops was curlin in on theyself
goin brown wit rot and how we prayed for rain
day in and out we prayed and
when it came it was a over-answered prayer
fields was flooded, water in every row,
black clouds seem like they was mockin
all us lookin up up with sorrowful faces
cuz we ain't understandin the nature of prayer
or anything callin itself GOD.

and i be wonderin now if freedom would be like that flood.
smotherin everythin inside it
i'm thinkin that's what a answered prayer
looks like . . .

a flood.
and God (or somethin like it)
mockin you and the way you
asked for it.

A Wizard and His Magic, Nothing More

And this is where the conundrum is.
I could, for the sake of entertainment,
Spin a proper tale to seduce the eye
And explode reason,

To tantalize the flesh
With an indifferent hand,
To see it flayed and hanging
From itself like wet sheets on the line
And offer no feeling wider
Than a sigh . . .

Ah but what a notion!
To play inside the bodies
Of savages
To find out the machinery

To *know* the mileage
Of flesh
And how does one do that
Except to flay it too?

No Magic, No How

that's when i take down
my own dumb heart . . .
right there
where Massa-Doctor say
i a mule wit a few
more miles left
to a slaver
stopped by for water
on his way to
someplace,

right there
right there
when Massa-Doctor look
right past the
way i hurt
to say
she a tough ole gal,
can take a mighty lickin'

right there
right there
i scoop out the little
bit of woman left and
let her ghosted bones
litter the creek bed
not enough of her

left even for rememberin
that's best.
no baby.
busted womb.
blood and shit and
Massa-Doctor's   prayer less ness
what i gotta do Jesus to
get out myself?
huh?
what i gotta do to
junk this here body.
tell me quick lawd.
i'm listenin
i's ready . . .

THE DOCTOR FIGURES IT OUT

Jubilee!
I say it because it is so.
Jubilee! A great day indeed!
How fine it is to author the cure
For a woman's tempestuous machinery
The ungodly nature of her composition
The one curse that can be undone
With the right hands
The right scalpel . . .
Ha!

The womb is so easily
Unfastened
The blood corsage
The ripening
The withering

Watch these hands
Fix what God
Could not
The twisted knots
Of a woman's mad body

Understood now
Through the snarling yawp of
Unblessed flesh,
The rotten fruit
The dying seed
Of one ordinary
Negro woman.

THE DOCTOR GIVES HER OPIUM AFTER

i dream sometimes.
me, but big and standin.
i got all my magic wit me
and ain't no noise i'm
waitin on and betsey and
lucy there too, gigglin girls
showin all they teeth
with full hands
and we matter to somebody
and got babies we can keep
who ain't dead and in the ground
buried out by the pond
and i know how to dance and keep my own
music and folk keep sayin *Sing Anarcha sing!*
and i pull a tune out and we twirl and put our
hands together and i tell god everything
with my dancin feet clattering laughter rain sometimes
white gloves, lace too, and sky and stars i can pull down
'round my neck
a holy place . . . the invention of love.

CONNIPTION

devil come wit two hands
like men do 'cept he
ain't got to pretend
he comin in the name of progress–

he get to be what he is
that ole ornery angel
what fell from heaven
on account of his own vanity

preacher say the devil is a liar
what about God then?

promising salvation long as you
let a white man kill you first
without makin no sounds
when he pull you under his
hot hands   hot hot hands

i blaspheme outright
cuz God don't speak to me
he ain't listenin or he dead, one or the other
either way all i got left

is silence . . .
the kind big enough to die in you hear me Jesus?

if you are in fact who they say you are

why you and yo daddy nowhere
to be found when i'm on my back?

heaven must be insurrection.

now that is something i can pray to.
hell is not knowin how to die.

First Is Last: How the Doctor Sees It

The other gals have folded mostly
Against their own curse-bitten flesh
But Anarcha's pluck is something else!

That gal you can split open, expose
The rind and she will shudder sure,
But she will stick and that has made
All the difference.

I am close now.
Oh dreadful body
Oh blessed body

I will do this work
To disturb the frailty
God himself designed for
The untethered bodies
Of woman.

I call it miracle.
I call it way-making.
Call it alchemy, then.
The oldest ritual

Watch me tend the upturned earth and
Pull the dead from
Unmarked graves
Watch me chase down

The blood and tell it to stillness.
This is the kind of love only
Invention can create.

And like anything else
There are losses

Sacrifice is a greedy ancestor
Clamoring for attention–

I'll listen.

First Is Last: How Anarcha Sees It

sun up this morning
like something raw
and full wit itself

and me:

me: bloodwaterbonespit

un-familied,

let the lord take these scraps
and let the lord be the *lord* . . .

let him take me
stripped and flayed
bone-bare, ragged, heavy

this thick, thick blood
this dream of iron and rope and
massa's hands behind me
fizzled down to nuthin
i need to remember

heaven's how i get away
i can believe in it if it means
        i get to leave

so let the lord be the *lord*

let him give me my mouth
new hands   new legs   no fever
maybe see my son?
maybe know him for myself?
maybe put the sun in my mouth
chew it up til i'm light all over
wouldn't that be something?

so take me lord . . .
this dust   this unremarkable dust
and do miracles with it . . .
some great and wonderful
thing with what i been and what i been through

do it lord . . . *unspell me. unspell me.*

A DEDICATION

I am still reeling from the possessive nature of ancestral writing. I am still humbled by elegy and the potential it holds to re-flesh the bones. I still tremble under the weight of history. The ships that carried folk I borrow bone and blood from to places they never imagined, where their suffering was bottomless. It is quite something to know they sizzle up through us and announce themselves still. Memory is aggressive. And long. And sometimes inherited. I elect to chase it down whenever possible. I intend to participate in as many resurrections as I can. That said, I am in debt to many people and you should know their names. Thank you to my children: Salih, Najah, Amir, and Igi. You all hold a mighty space for me to empty out and get my crazy done and conjure when and where I am able and I am so honored to be your mama. Thank you to THE matriarch, my own mother, Professor Jacquelyn Benton, for being so holy and for keeping me tethered to my body in the course of writing *Anarcha*. I would also like to thank Rachel McKibbens, Mahogany Browne, Jennifer Falu, and Letitia Salazar Monk. Womenfolk who unapologetically perform their own magic in the world in ways that have, directly and indirectly, saved my life. Women who remind me of how urgent sisterhood is and what salve it offers. And oh my goodness thank you to Tyehimba Jess for the work he does in the world, for his brilliance, his exquisite introduction to this book, and for seeing me. I'm so honored I can't even language it adequately. Thank you, Tye-himba. Thank you for choosing *Anarcha* . . . for choosing me. And lastly, though my grandmother is no longer here, I have to thank her too. Because I have known women, matriarchal moon-struck, magic women who have gifted me with story and backbone and a breadcrumb trail to follow when I lose my way. This book is for the ones who remain nameless; remain anonymous; remain unlit and unblessed. May this work be a breadcrumb trail to follow. May it lead us into remembrance of those we lost. May it give them back the benefit of their names.

—DOMINIQUE CHRISTINA

ABOUT THE AUTHOR

DOMINIQUE CHRISTINA was born in Denver, was educated at the University of the Pacific and the University of Arkansas, and was a classroom teacher at the secondary and post-secondary levels for ten years. She was part of the team that won the National Poetry Slam Championship in 2011, and she was named (as Dominique Ashaheed) Women of the World Slam Champion in 2012 and 2014. She is the author of *The Bones, the Breaking, the Balm* (2014), *They Are All Me* (2015), and *This Is Woman's Work* (2015) and has been a featured speaker at hundreds of colleges and universities nationally and internationally.

TYEHIMBA JESS was born in Detroit and studied at the University of Chicago and New York University. He is the author of *Olio*, winner of the 2017 Pulitzer Prize for Poetry, and *leadbelly*, winner of the 2004 National Poetry Series. Jess has received a National Endowment for the Arts Fellowship, a Provincetown Fine Arts Work Center Fellowship, and a Whiting Award.